Do You See What I See?

3D Christmas Surprises from Magic Eye

3D Illusions by N.E. Thing Enterprises

Andrews and McMeel

A Universal Press Syndicate Company

Kansas City

ISBN: 0-8362-7018-5

ATTENTION: SCHOOLS AND BUSINESSES

Andrews and McMeel books are available at quantity discounts with bulk purchase for educational, business, or sales promotional use. For information, please write to: Special Sales Department, Andrews and McMeel, 4900 Main Street, Kansas City, Missouri 64112.

INTRODUCTION

The magic of Christmas springs to life for good boys and girls of all ages with these gifts you open with your eyes. Our latest collection of goodies is chock-full of surprises including the world's first double-decker illusions, found on pages 5 and 17. Each page actually contains *two* totally different hidden images! The first hidden image is seen in the normal way (as described on the next page), with your eyes aimed at a point beyond the page. The second image can be seen by diverging your eyes even more, with the eyes aimed at a point far beyond the page. Instead of fusing the repeating patterns that are next to each other, every other pattern should be fused. For those of you with experienced Magic Eyes, this will be a new challenge. Neophytes should not attempt this without super vision!

We hope that you'll share these gifts with family and friends throughout the season . . .

HAPPY HOLIDAYS!

NOTE: Pages 31 and 32 of this book provide a key that shows the 3D picture that you'll see when you find and train your Magic Eye. There are some images in the book that do not contain a hidden picture; instead the various repeated objects will seem to float in space at different distances when viewed correctly. These images are on pages 7, 10, 16, 19, and 25. For many, they are easier to see than the other pictures.

VIEWING TECHNIQUES

Learning to use your Magic Eye is a bit like learning to ride a bicycle. Once you get it, it gets easier and easier. If possible, try to learn to use your Magic Eye in a quiet, meditative time and place. Although Magic Eye is great fun at work and other entertaining social situations, those are not often the best places to learn. If you don't get it in two or three minutes, wait until another, quieter time. For most people, it's a real effort to figure out how to use the Magic Eye.

In all of the Magic Eye images, you'll note a repeating pattern. In order to "see" a Magic Eye picture, two things must happen. First, you must get one eye to look at a point in the image, while the other eye looks at the same point in the next pattern. Second, you must hold your eyes in that position long enough for the marvelous structures in your brain to decode the 3D information that has been coded into the repeating patterns by our computer programs.

There are two methods of viewing our 3D images: Crossing your eyes and diverging your eyes. Crossing your eyes occurs when you aim your eyes at a point between your eyes and an image; diverging your eyes occurs when your eyes are aimed at a point beyond the image.

All of our pictures are designed to be seen by diverging the eyes. It is also possible to see them with the cross-eyed method, but all the depth information comes out backward! If we intend to show an airplane flying in front of a cloud using the diverging eye method, you will see an airplane-shaped hole cut into the cloud if you look at it with the cross-eyed method. Once you learn one method, try the other. It's fun, but most people do better with one or the other. We think that most people prefer the diverging method. Another possibility is to diverge the eyes twice as far as is needed to see the image. In this case, a weird, more complex version of the intended object is seen.

One last note before you start. Although this technique is safe, and even potentially helpful to your eyes, don't overdo it! Straining will not help, and could cause you to feel uncomfortable. That is not the way to proceed. Ask your nephew or the paper girl to give you some help; they'll probably be able to do it in ten seconds. The key is to relax and let the image come to you.

METHOD ONE

Hold the image so that it touches your nose. Let the eyes relax, and stare vacantly off into space, as if looking through the image. Relax and become comfortable with the idea of observing the image, without looking at it. When you are relaxed and not crossing your eyes, move the page slowly away from your face. Perhaps an inch every two or three seconds. Keep looking through the page. Stop at a comfortable reading distance and keep staring. The most discipline is needed when something starts to "come in," because at that moment you'll instinctively try to look at the page rather than looking through it. If you look at it, start again.

METHOD TWO

The cover of this book is shiny; hold it in such a way that you can identify a reflection. For example, hold it under an overhead lamp so that it catches its light. Simply look at the object you see reflected, and continue to stare at it with a fixed gaze. After several seconds, you'll perceive depth, followed by the 3D image, which will develop almost like an instant photo!

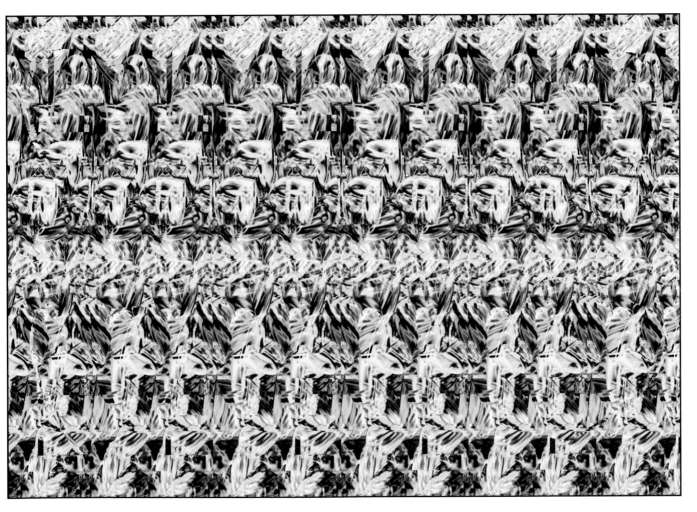

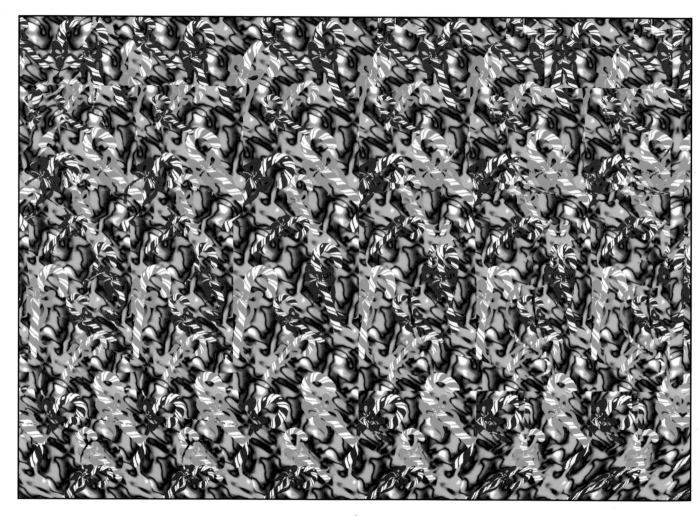

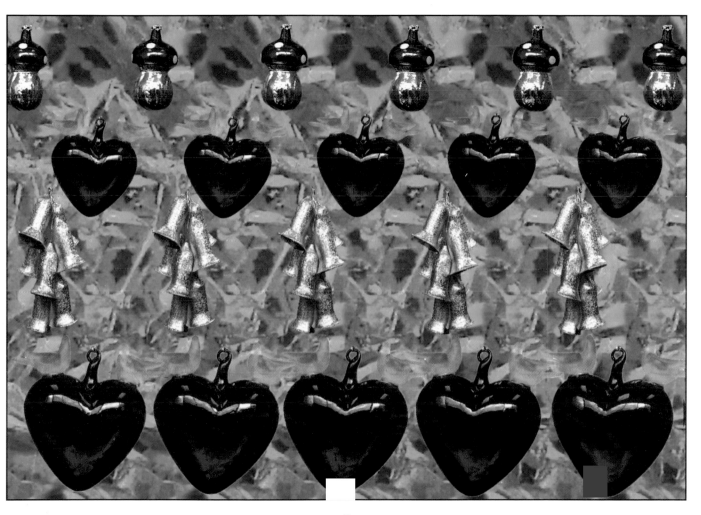

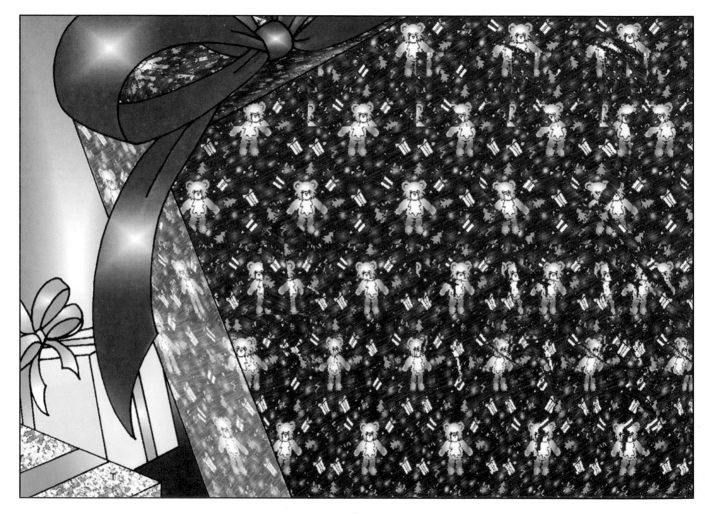

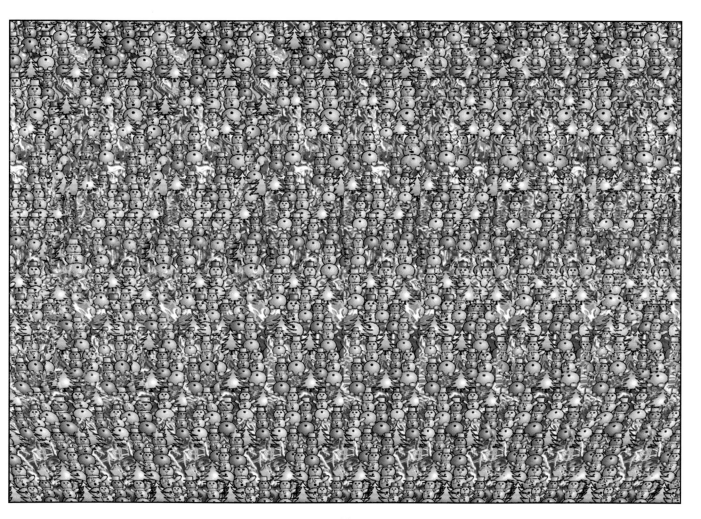

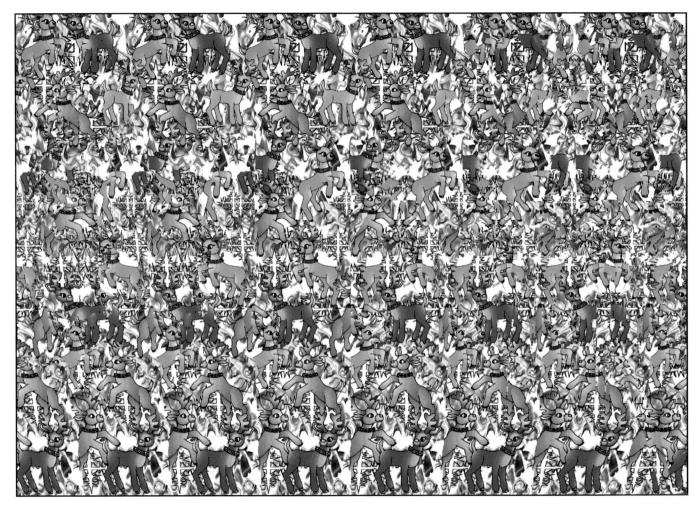

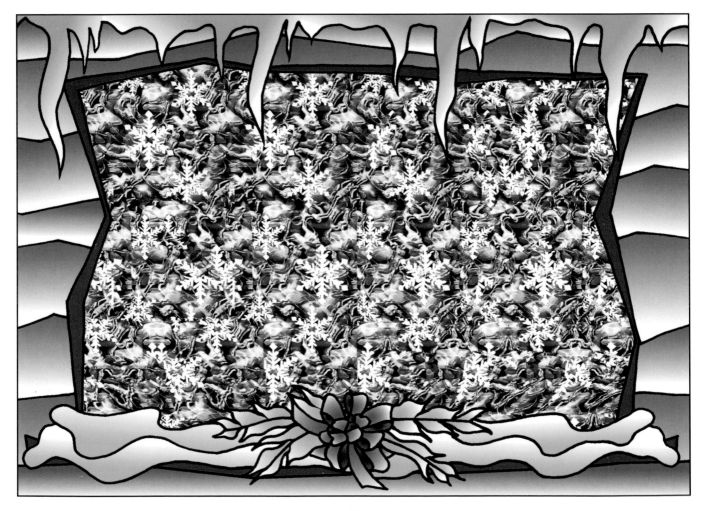

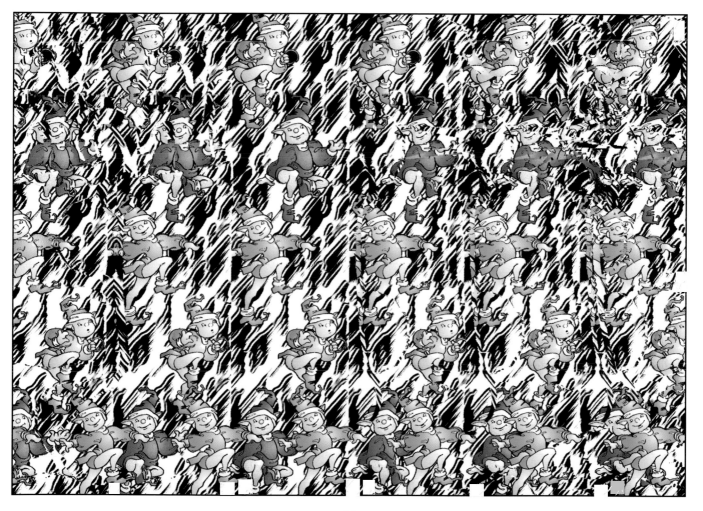

15

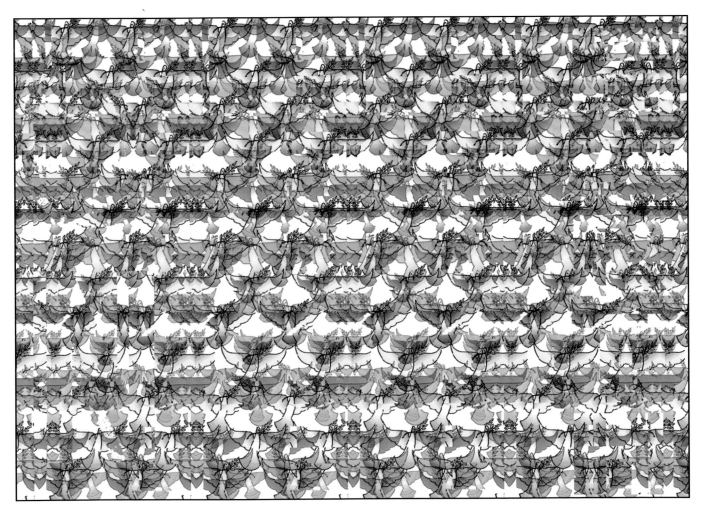

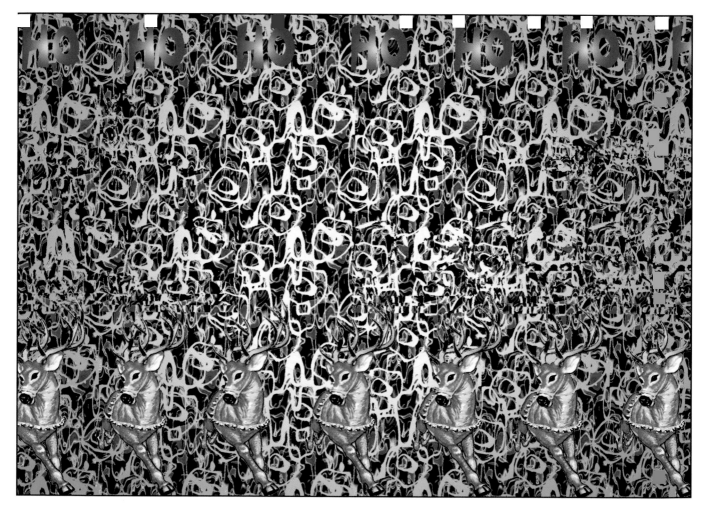

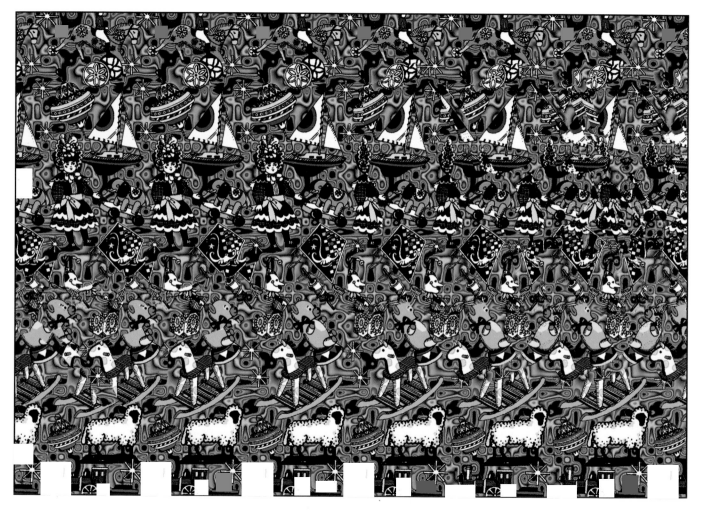

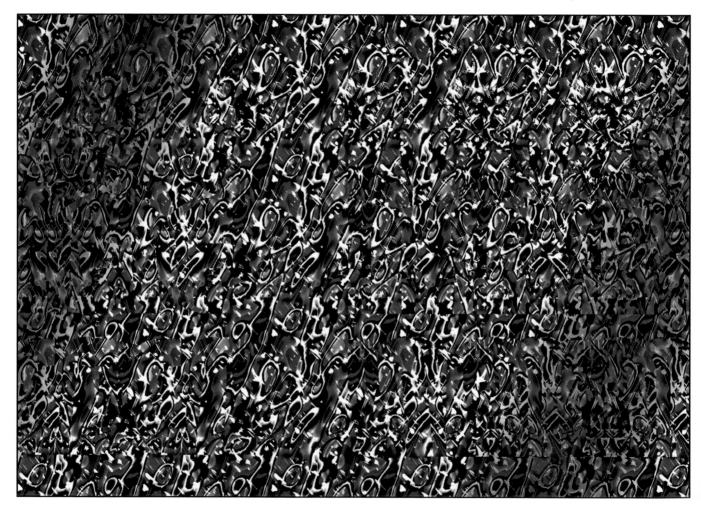

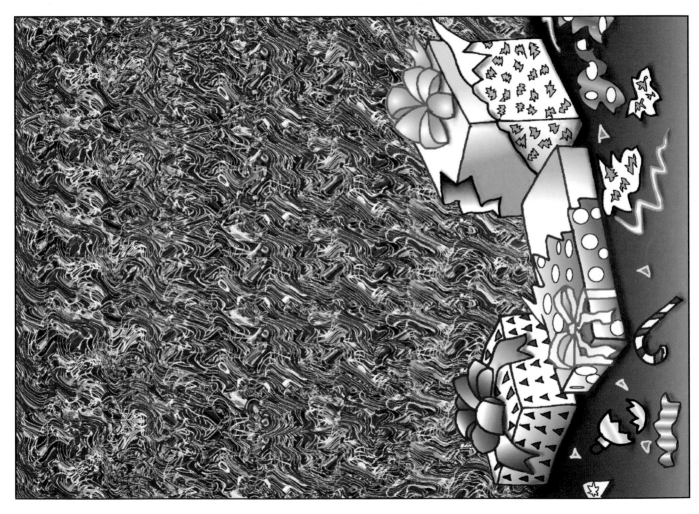

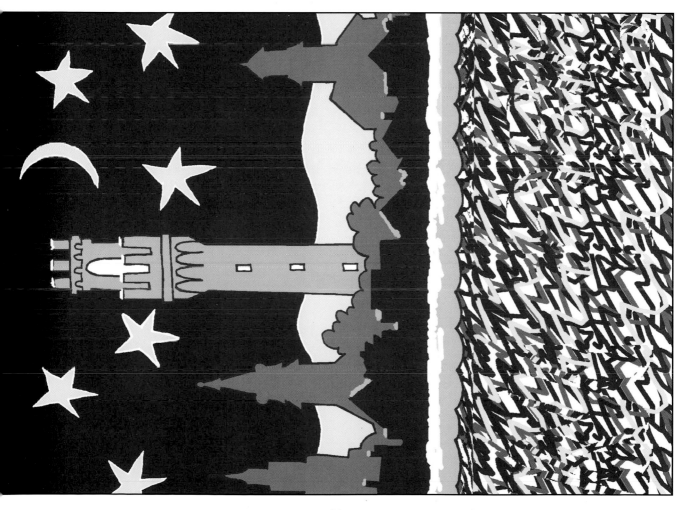

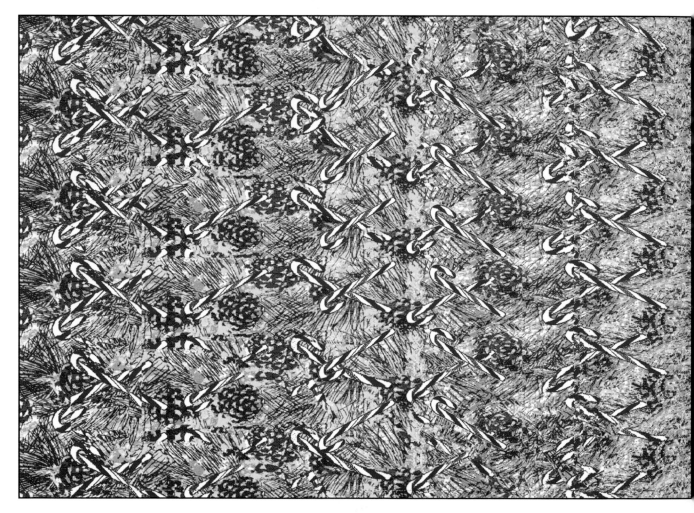

30

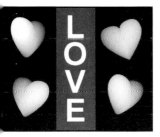

*Page 5 I Love Christmas

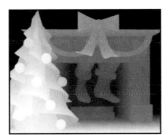

Page 6 Feet First

Page 8 Bearly Opened

Page 9 Jingle Bells

Page 11 Coolman

Page 12 Reindeer Games

Page 13 Holly Wreath

Page 14 The Night Shift

Page 15 Stocking Stuffers

*Page 17 Peace on Earth

Page 18 North Pole Express

Page 20 Silent Night

*For instructions on double-decker images, see introduction.

Page 21 Santa's Favorite

Page 22 Toyland

Page 23 Saint Nick

Page 24 Season's Greetings

Page 26 Sweet Dreams

Page 27 Heaven Above

Page 28 Bad Boy

Page 29 Cape Cod Christmas

Page 30 Tree-D